YOU CHOOSE BOOKS™

THE BATTLE OF THE
ALAMO

An Interactive History Adventure

by Amie Jane Leavitt

Consultant:
Mickie Ross
Adult Program Coordinator
Texas State Historical Association
Austin, Texas

Capstone
press®

Mankato, Minnesota

You Choose Books are published by Capstone Press,
151 Good Counsel Drive, P.O. Box 669, Mankato, Minnesota 56002.
www.capstonepress.com

Library of Congress Cataloging-in-Publication Data
Leavitt, Amie Jane.
    The Battle of the Alamo : an interactive history adventure / by Amie Jane Leavitt.
    p. cm. — (You choose books)
    Includes bibliographical references and index.
    ISBN-13: 978-1-4296-1354-5 (hardcover) ISBN-13: 978-1-4296-1761-1 (softcover)
    ISBN-10: 1-4296-1354-8 (hardcover)   ISBN-10: 1-4296-1761-6 (softcover)
    1. Alamo (San Antonio, Tex.) — Siege, 1836 — Juvenile literature. I. Title. II. Series.
F390.L35 2008
976.4'03 — dc22   2007036206

Summary: Describes the Battle of the Alamo in March 1836 as Mexican soldiers overwhelmed
the Texian Alamo defenders and explains what the battle symbolizes today. The reader's choices reveal
historical details from the perspective of a Mexican soldier and a Texian rebel.

Editorial Credits

Heather Adamson and Carrie A. Braulick, editors; Juliette Peters, set designer; Gene Bentdahl, book
    designer; Danielle Ceminsky, illustrator; Wanda Winch, photo researcher

Photo Credits

Alan C. Huffines (Author) and Gary Zaboly (Illustrator), "Blood of Noble Men: The Alamo Siege and
Battle (Eakin 1999), 17, 24, 34, 37, 47, 53, 65, 75, 95; The Bridgeman Art Library International/Private
Collection, Peter Newark American Pictures/David (Davy) Crockett (1786-1836) with his hunting dogs in
1836 (colour litho), American School, (19th century), 62; The Bridgeman Art Library International/Private
Collection, Roger-Viollet, Paris/A Courier Enters the Besieged Fort of Alamo, San Antonio, February-
March 1836 during the War of Texas (oil on canvas), American School, (19th century), 89; Capstone
Press, 19; Corbis/Bettmann, 99; Courtesy of The Sam Houston Regional Library and Research Center,
Liberty, Texas, Jean Houston Baldwin Collection, 103; CROCKETT'S LAST SUNRISE - The Alamo,
1836 © MarkChurms.com 1997, All Rights Reserved, 69; Daughters of the Republic of Texas Library, ID
#SC95.342, 104; Daughters of the Republic of Texas Library/Alamo Collection, San Antonio, Texas, ID
#SC97.024, 97; Daughters of the Republic of Texas Library/Alamo Collection, San Antonio, Texas/San
Jacinto Association Collection/Hugo D. Pohl (1878-1960), William Barret Travis, ID #SC97.004, 60; Gary
S. Zaboly, Illustrator, 73, 84; The Granger Collection, New York, 12, 50; Joe LeMonnier, www.mapartist.
com, 67; North Wind Picture Archives, 6, 28; Old Army Press, 15; REMEMBER THE ALAMO,
REMEMBER GOLIAD! Battle of San Jacinto 1836 © MarkChurms.com 2003. All Rights Reserved, 105;
Shutterstock/Sally Scott, 100; Siege of the Alamo, Courtesy of the State Preservation Board, Austin, TX;
Accession ID: CHA 1989.383; Original Artwork by Markos, Lajos / 1917-1993; Photographer: Eric Beggs,
1/17/01, pre conservation, cover; SuperStock, Inc., 55; The Texas State Preservation Board/Sequin, Juan
Nepomuceno 1989.96 Original Painting by: Wright, Thomas Jefferson / 1798-1846 Photographer: Perry
Huston 7/28/95 post conservation, 79; "You May Take Our Lives, But You Will Never Take Our Freedom"
painting by Kirk Stirnweis, Stirnweis Studio, 57

1 2 3 4 5 6 13 12 11 10 09 08

TABLE OF CONTENTS

About Your Adventure

YOU are living in the early 1800s. Texas is part of Mexico. But you're not sure it will stay that way for long. New laws in Mexico have enraged some Texians so much that they are fighting for Texas' independence. Will you fight for Texas' freedom or against it?

In this book, you'll explore how the choices people made meant the difference between life and death. The events you'll experience happened to real people.

Chapter One sets the scene. Then you choose which path to read. Follow the directions at the bottom of each page. The choices you make will change your outcome. After you finish one path, go back and read the others for new perspectives and more adventures.

YOU CHOOSE the path you take through history.

Santa Anna became the
president of Mexico in 1834.

CHAPTER 1

TAKING SIDES OVER TEXAS

It's December 9, 1835. The streets of San Antonio, Texas, are filled with excitement. After four days of battle, the Mexican leader, General Martín Perfecto de Cos, has surrendered. The townspeople of San Antonio cheer when the Mexican Army marches out of the city. Soon the news of the surrender spreads to other Texas citizens, or Texians.

The Mexicans feel ashamed for losing to soldiers they consider to be backwoods frontiersmen. In 1821, they won their independence from Spain. And that was against a professionally trained army.

Turn the page.

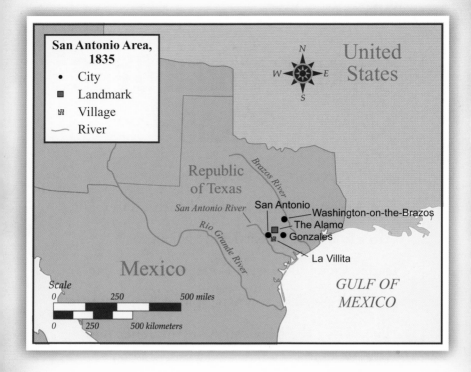

If the Texians think they have won the fight, they are wrong. The Mexican soldiers know they'll be back to reclaim their honor.

Across Mexico, many citizens wonder what the fighting is about. After all, Texas is part of Mexico. And even though many Texians are from the United States, most have become Mexican citizens. They always got along with the government. Why are they now fighting against Mexico?

The problems started soon after Antonio López de Santa Anna became president in 1834. After Mexico became free of Spain in 1821, the new leaders wrote a constitution. This set of laws protected the rights of the people and gave them the right to vote. But Santa Anna thought the constitution was making Mexico weak. He decided to make laws of his own. Under these harsher laws, citizens had fewer rights. Most Mexicans went along with the new laws without complaining.

Turn the page.

But many Texians felt differently about Santa Anna's laws. They came from the United States. They were used to having more of a say in their government. The Texians worried that giving up a few rights now could mean losing more before long. Some Texian leaders were so angry that they started a rebellion. They wanted Texas to break free of Mexico and become an independent country.

News of the rebellion in Texas made it back to Mexico City. Santa Anna was furious. How dare these rebels try to steal Mexico's land? In late 1835, he sent General Cos to deal with the Texians. The Mexicans and Texians fought many battles. But after this last battle on December 9, the Mexicans were forced out of Texas.

Now, Mexican citizens all around you are making difficult choices. Many Mexican citizens support Santa Anna. They believe Texas should remain with Mexico. Others are choosing to fight with the Texian rebels. What will you decide?

→ To serve in Santa Anna's army, turn to page **13**.

→ To fight with the Texians, turn to page **61**.

In the early 1800s, many Mexicans lived in adobe homes, which are made of sun-dried bricks.

CHAPTER 2

Life in Santa Anna's Army

You were born in Mexico. You would never fight against your own country. Your family is here. And although you work hard for a living, you believe Mexico is a fine place to call home.

Santa Anna's army has some professional soldiers. But Santa Anna needs more men to fight with him. One day, Santa Anna's officers come to your village looking for volunteers to join the army. Few men want to join. They explain that their families need them. But the officers take no excuses. They say every man must fight in Santa Anna's army.

Turn the page.

Like many of your neighbors, you would rather stay with your family. But since you have no choice, you go with the officers to the army camp.

Early one morning in late December, you travel north with the huge army from the city of San Luis Potosi. As you look behind your shoulder, it seems like the trail of soldiers never ends. You are headed toward San Antonio, Texas. You aren't looking forward to the long trip. It's more than 400 miles to San Antonio.

Even though it's winter, the sun feels warm as you march across the desert. But after a few days, the weather turns cold. It's unusual for the weather to be this cold in Mexico. One evening, you are surprised to see heavy snow falling. You're glad you brought your poncho. You huddle under this thick, wool cape to keep warm.

Mexican officers in the cavalry carried muskets on horseback.

When you awaken, 15 inches of snow cover the ground. A fellow soldier then tells you some terrible news. Several other soldiers have frozen to death during the night. After burying the dead soldiers, the army continues marching.

One evening, you study your musket. You don't know how you'll protect yourself in battle with this gun. You've never shot one before. You hope the officers will have time to train you before your first battle.

Turn the page.

Every evening, you receive your food rations. At first, you were given 1 pound of meat, some beans, and corn. But that has changed. Little food is left. Now each day's ration is a small, dry biscuit called hardtack. You can barely choke down the dry bread, but you know your body needs every bit of energy it can get.

One January evening, you notice General Santa Anna feasting on a huge meal from a crystal dish. His uniform is decorated with shiny war medals, and his long gold saber glistens. "I wish the soldiers had such good things to eat," you mutter to yourself.

The Mexicans encountered swollen rivers during their march to San Antonio.

Finally, the army reaches the Rio Grande River in February. Before your unit crosses the river, your commander shows the group how to fire the cannons and muskets.

⇢ *To learn how to fire a musket, turn to page **18**.*

⇢ *To learn how to fire a cannon, turn to page **25**.*

You watch carefully as the captain shows your group how to load the musket. It isn't as simple as you had thought. You hope you'll be able to load your musket quickly enough in battle.

Later in the day, you cross the Rio Grande River and continue on to San Antonio. Finally, on February 23, you arrive.

"Many of the townspeople have left," the captain says. "But the Texians are hiding in the old mission." He points across the river. "Spanish missionaries lived there years ago. It's called the Alamo."

You squint to see the mission. Some buildings don't even have roofs! And the stone walls don't look very strong. You're glad you aren't hiding in there.

Boom! Suddenly, the earth shakes beneath your feet as a cannon from the Alamo fires.

San Antonio was a growing city in the early 1800s.

"The Texians must be responding to Santa Anna's flag," the captain says. A red flag waves from a nearby church. "Santa Anna wants the rebels to surrender. The flag means he will take no prisoners after a battle. It doesn't sound like the Texians are willing to give up yet."

Turn the page.

That evening, a group of men leaves to set up a roadblock. Santa Anna wants to stop the Texians from getting help from nearby towns. Your commander is also asking for a drummer to join the band.

↠ To set up a roadblock, go to page **21**.

↠ To join the band, turn to page **40**.

You follow the captain down a dusty road. After several miles, you see Santa Anna's cavalry. They've already arrived on horseback and are setting up camp.

You spend the next day on patrol at the roadblock. Your job is to stop anyone who approaches. But so far, nothing has happened. All you do is march up and down the road. You are bored doing the same thing over and over.

Later that evening, you hear hoofbeats. Two riders approach from San Antonio.

"Stop!" you yell.

One rider calls out a greeting in Spanish. Deciding they're part of your cavalry, you lower your musket.

Turn the page.

But the riders don't stop as you expect. Instead, they kick their spurs, whip their reins, and bolt down the road. As they race past, you realize they're Texians!

You aim your musket and fire. The cavalrymen mount their horses and chase after them. But it's too late. The rebels have already disappeared into the darkness.

"Santa Anna will be outraged at this!" the cavalry's leader shouts. "Those men are likely delivering messages to Texian leaders. You'd better pray they don't return with an army of rebels to help them!"

Later that night, your commander shouts an order. "The cavalry no longer wants our help," he barks. "We're leaving immediately."

You march all night long and arrive in San Antonio just before sunrise. When you get there, the commander asks for volunteers. A group is needed to march into La Villita. This small village of shacks is only 300 yards away from the Alamo. From there, he hopes to get a closer shot at the Texians. Another group is needed to build a bridge over the San Antonio River. You are eager to make up for your mistake at the roadblock. But which task will you choose?

→ To go to La Villita, turn to page 44.

→ To build the bridge, turn to page 49.

In the 1800s, soldiers used a long pole called a rammer (left of cannon) to load cannons.

"Follow me," the captain orders. He walks toward a group of cannons. "These cannons fire 9-pound balls," he says. "We also have 12-pounders. General Genoa's troops are pushing them across the desert."

The captain assigns every man a different job. He hands you a long wooden pole called a rammer. On one end is a lambskin sponge. You dip it into water and clean the cannon's muzzle. Then, you ram a cartridge of gunpowder into the opening. Other soldiers drop in the cannonball and place a fuse and rope inside the rear of the gun. The cannon is loaded.

Turn the page.

"Fire!" the captain orders. A soldier tugs the rope tight. Boom! Smoke rings rise as the ball whistles through the air.

"Good work, men," the captain says. "I need five men on my cannon crew. Step forward if I can count on you."

➤ To join the cannon crew, go to page 27.

➤ To return to your ranks, turn to page 30.

The captain welcomes you to the cannon crew. The next day, you cross the wide Rio Grande River and begin to push the heavy cannons across the desert.

On February 23, you reach San Antonio. It looks deserted. The residents must have fled when they heard the army was coming. Your crew sets up a battery by grouping four cannons together.

"Aim at those buildings," your commander shouts, pointing across the San Antonio River. "That's the Alamo. It's where the rebels are hiding."

Turn the page.

Texians fled to the Alamo because its tall walls provided some protection in an attack.

Later, you notice Santa Anna and other officers standing in a nearby church's bell tower. A soldier raises a flag. It's not the Mexican flag. It's just a piece of plain red fabric. But it is a signal.

"Santa Anna plans on fighting to the death," your captain says, as he points to the flag. "Santa Anna will take no prisoners."

Suddenly, you hear a loud cannon explosion. Smoke rises from the Alamo. The Texians saw the flag, and they don't plan to give up.

Seconds later, your commander races to the battery. "Fire one shot from each cannon," he says. "Santa Anna's orders!"

Your crew quickly prepares the cannon. Boom! Your cannon lobs a ball high into the air. You continue firing the cannons throughout the night. You're proud of how your battery has been working together.

The next evening, you see a group of men with shovels. They are leaving to dig trenches. Santa Anna wants the batteries moved closer to the Alamo.

➤ To dig the trenches, turn to page **36**.

➤ To keep firing the cannons, turn to page **45**.

Firing the cannon was exciting. But you want to be in the middle of the action as a regular soldier.

That night, a soldier approaches you. He was on your cannon crew earlier today.

"We should have learned to fire our muskets," he says. "Now we won't know how to defend ourselves in battle." He leans in closer and whispers. "Some of us are sneaking away tonight. We'll surely be killed in battle if we stay. Want to join us?"

You're shocked at his words. If these men are caught, they'll be punished. Even if they get away, they'll have to walk across the desert without supplies.

You've heard stories about attacks from Indian tribes in the area. What if Indians attack the men? Yet if you stay, you might not have any better luck in battle.

❧ To leave the army, turn to page **43**.

❧ To stay and fight, turn to page **32**.

"I am not a coward," you say. "I will stay and fight."

"Suit yourself," he mutters, walking away.

The next day, you cross the Rio Grande River and continue your march toward San Antonio. On February 23, you finally arrive. "The Texians are hiding out in the old mission called the Alamo," an officer says.

As you look at the buildings, your commander approaches. "Come with me to San Fernando Church," he says. "Santa Anna needs our help."

You follow him into the town. Santa Anna and his generals are waiting by the church's main door.

"Follow us to the top of the bell tower," your commander says.

At the top, you see the Alamo more clearly. A flag waves above it. It's not Mexico's flag. It must be the rebels' flag of independence.

Santa Anna spits in disgust. He thrusts a red flag into your hands. "Raise it," he yells. "It'll send a message to the traitors. If we go to battle, we'll fight them to the death."

Turn the page.

You fasten the flag to the pole and unfold it in the chilly breeze. Its red cloth contrasts with the clear blue sky behind it.

Santa Anna leads the group down the tower. Boom! An explosion nearly knocks you off your feet. You stumble outside. An officer darts toward Santa Anna. "The rebels shot their cannon after we raised the flag," he says.

Mexican soldiers raised a flag from San Fernando Church to send a message to the Texians.

"Send them four shots in response!" Santa Anna shouts to his generals. "The battle has begun!"

You return to camp. That night, you see some soldiers walking by with shovels. They are going to dig trenches so the batteries can be moved closer to the Alamo. You think about joining them. Just then, your commander walks by. "I'm looking for a drummer for the regimental band," he says.

➤ To dig trenches, turn to page **36**.

➤ To join the band, turn to page **40**.

You grab a shovel and follow the men. "Start digging here," the captain orders.

Digging the trench in the rocky soil is hard work. You quickly become tired, hungry, and thirsty. But there's no time to stop. The captain orders everyone to work faster. "*Rápido!*" he shouts.

Just before sunrise, you return to camp. You rest a few hours before the cannons start firing again.

The next evening, your commander walks by just as you are preparing to dig trenches again. "We need to cut off the water supply to the Alamo," he says. "Without water, the Texians might surrender."

➛ To keep digging trenches, turn to page **38**.

➛ To cut off the water supply, go to page **37**.

The Mexican soldiers dug trenches so their cannons could move closer to the Alamo.

You are tired of digging into the hard, rocky soil. Maybe cutting off the water supply will be easier work. With a few other soldiers, you walk to a long, narrow ditch filled with water. You quickly dig up dirt and shovel it into the ditch. By dawn, no more water flows into the Alamo.

Later in the morning, your commander tells you to continue digging trenches.

Turn the page.

Night after night, you continue digging. Your hands start to blister and your back aches. But you are making progress. The cannon crews are getting closer and closer to the Alamo.

On March 3, your commander calls a meeting. "I need two crews. One will build a bridge over the San Antonio River. The other will build some ladders," he says.

→ *To build ladders, go to page* **39**.

→ *To build a bridge, turn to page* **49**.

That evening and throughout the next day, you strap boards together with twine. "These ladders can only mean one thing," someone says. "We're charging the Alamo on foot — and soon."

"But I thought we weren't going to attack without the 12-pounders," you reply.

"Santa Anna doesn't care how many of us get killed. He wants to attack with or without the big guns."

You spend a restless day back at camp. At 1:00 in the morning on March 6, your commander barks his order. "Get into line, but be quiet. This is a surprise attack. The first group will carry the ladders. The second will run with muskets."

To charge in the first wave, turn to page **52**.

To charge in the second wave, turn to page **54**.

"I can play a drum," you tell your commander. He shows you where the band is practicing. You hook the drum to your side, pick up a pair of sticks, and tap the drum's hard surface.

You are ordered to play battle tunes as the cannons fire. And each night, from evening until dawn, the cannons fire ball after ball at the Alamo. Your tired arms somehow find a way to keep beating the drum.

On the evening of March 5, you overhear two officers talking outside their tents.

"Santa Anna has ordered an attack tomorrow morning."

"He isn't going to wait for the larger cannons to arrive?"

"No. He is tired of waiting. He doesn't care how many of his soldiers are killed in battle."

You feel sick. You didn't think Santa Anna would fight without his best cannons. You know that as a band member, you're safer than other soldiers. Still, you fear for the lives of your friends.

You're awakened at 1:00 in the morning. You join the band members in the center of the camp. You must keep quiet until the attack starts. Santa Anna wants to surprise the Texians.

Turn the page.

It's nearly daybreak when the commander sounds the call. "Charge!" he shouts. The foot soldiers race toward the Alamo. Some men carry ladders so they can climb over the Alamo's 12-foot walls. Others clutch their muskets.

Suddenly, the Texians open fire. Many Mexican soldiers are killed instantly. Others lie wounded on the ground. You watch the battle in horror. Then you see more foot soldiers loading their guns. They are preparing to charge the Alamo in the attack's second wave. Suddenly, a thought crosses your mind. Maybe you should join them. You know you're safer with the band, but your fellow soldiers need your help.

➤ To stay with the band, turn to page **51**.

➤ To charge the Alamo, turn to page **54**.

You know it's risky to leave the army, but you decide to take your chances anyway. One of your friends decides to leave too.

You wait for the captain to fall asleep. Then you creep to the edge of the camp. The rest of the group is waiting. You quietly sneak past the guards.

As you run across the desert, your friend trips in the darkness. "Help me!" he cries. "My leg feels broken!"

The rest of the men keep running. If you stop to help, you could get caught by the guards. But can you leave your friend alone?

→ To help your friend, turn to page **56**.

→ To catch up with the group, turn to page **58**.

You march with the men to La Villita. From the village, you can see the Texians standing on the Alamo's walls. Suddenly, they open fire. Fellow soldiers near you fall to the ground. You dive for cover behind one of the shacks. Your hands shake as you struggle to load your weapon. Finally, you aim at the Alamo and fire. As you hurry to reload, you feel a horrible, burning pain. Enemy fire has hit you. You drop your musket and slump against the shack's wall. It's all over for you. You have given your life for Mexico.

44

THE END

To follow another path, turn to page 11.
To read the conclusion, turn to page 101.

Each night, you fire the cannons while the band plays battle tunes. A crew continues to dig trenches. After several days, the batteries have moved closer to the Alamo. You're now within 200 yards of its walls.

On the morning of March 5, you overhear two officers talking.

"We can't wait for the 12-pound cannons to arrive," one says. "Santa Anna told the generals last night. We're charging the Alamo early tomorrow morning."

"What?" the other replies. "With the 12-pounders, we can easily break down the walls. With less protection, the Texians will likely surrender. If we charge now, we'll be running right into their bullets."

Turn the page.

"That's what the generals told him. But Santa Anna doesn't care. He wants a big victory. And he wants it now!"

After hearing this news, you feel sick. Your stomach tightens in fear.

The next morning, you're awakened at 1:00. You take your post at the cannon and watch the foot soldiers prepare for battle.

Near daybreak, the commander calls the charge. "*Arriba*!" he shouts. The foot soldiers burst forward toward the Alamo.

"Fire the cannons," the captain orders. Boom! You fire ball after ball toward the Alamo.

By March 6, the Mexican cannons were close enough to cause serious damage to the Alamo.

The Texians return fire. Everywhere you look, Mexican soldiers are falling, either killed or wounded. The rest keep charging forward.

47

Turn the page.

Soon, the first wave of men reaches the Alamo's walls. The Texians fight to keep them out. But it's no use. There are hundreds more Mexican soldiers than Texians. It's not long before the Mexican soldiers are inside the Alamo.

The battle continues for almost an hour. Flashes of light fill the early morning sky. Finally, the last shot is fired. You're grateful you're still alive. Many of your friends aren't so lucky.

48

THE END

To follow another path, turn to page 11.
To read the conclusion, turn to page 101.

The San Antonio River twists through the town like a snake. The bridge will be built over the part nearest the Alamo. You know it'll be dangerous working so close to the Texians during daylight.

Wagons of timber sit near the river. You help unload. As you place the last piece on the ground, you hear gunfire. The Texians are shooting right at you!

You crouch behind one of the wagon's tall wooden wheels. Bullets whiz past you. A soldier next to you tries to load his musket. Before he can finish, a bullet hits him. He falls wounded at your feet.

Turn the page.

Thousands of Mexican soldiers stormed the Alamo just before dawn on March 6, 1836.

You take off running. You hope to get out of the Texans' shooting range. Your heart races and your head pounds. You have never run so fast in your life. Just when you think you're safe, a sharp pain strikes your side. You slump to the earth. Your life ends right there in the shadow of the Alamo.

THE END

To follow another path, turn to page 11.
To read the conclusion, turn to page 101.

You long to see your friends and family again. And you know staying in the band will give you the best chance of doing so.

"Start playing 'Deguello'," the commander orders. It's Santa Anna's favorite battle tune, but not yours. The tune reminds you only of hatred and death.

Your stomach sickens as you watch the battle. Mexicans climb the walls, and the Texians try to fight them off. But the foot soldiers keep charging. Soon hundreds of Mexicans are inside the Alamo's walls.

After an hour, the battle is over, and your side has won. But it was at a great cost. Hundreds of your fellow soldiers have perished.

THE END

To follow another path, turn to page 11.
To read the conclusion, turn to page 101.

Near daybreak, the captain shouts his command, "Charge!" Your crew lifts the heavy ladder and starts running.

It's difficult to run while carrying the ladder. You press the ladder snugly against your chest and try not to stumble.

As you approach the Alamo, the Texian riflemen start shooting in your direction. Their bullets whiz past you. You have nowhere to hide.

"I can't die here in this battle," you decide. You drop your section of the ladder and run toward the river.

"Keep charging," someone shouts. But you do not obey. You just keep running away from the battle. You approach a rickety bridge and dive underneath it for safety.

Mexican soldiers used tall ladders to climb the Alamo's 12-foot walls.

You watch the men charging the Alamo. Gunfire lights the sky. Soon, the fighting is over. As you sneak back to camp, you see hundreds of men lying dead on the ground. Even though you feel like a coward for running away, you're grateful you're not one of the dead.

THE END

To follow another path, turn to page 11.
To read the conclusion, turn to page 101.

You watch the men with ladders race toward the Alamo. Many of them are hit by the Texians' bullets and fall to the ground.

Soon, it's time for the second wave to attack. You clutch your musket tightly as you sprint across the battlefield. Bullets shot by the Texians pepper your fellow soldiers. A ladder crew falls down right in front of you.

"Help me lift this ladder," you yell. "We have to get it to the wall."

Three soldiers stop to help. The ladder is heavy and awkward to carry. But you keep going. You finally brace your ladder against one of the Alamo's walls and race up it.

Texian defenders inside the Alamo fought bravely, but the Mexicans overwhelmed them.

Once inside, you are face-to-face with a Texian rifleman. He aims and fires. You collapse to the hard earth below. You take your last breath lying on the dusty ground.

THE END

To follow another path, turn to page 11.
To read the conclusion, turn to page 101.

You know you're risking your life. But you can't leave your friend.

"Climb onto my back," you order. He's heavy, but you're determined to carry him. You must hurry. If you stay here much longer, you'll be caught. It's hard to see in the dark, and you stumble several times.

Suddenly, you hear gunfire. "Stop!" someone shouts. You dive behind a bush. The guards fire their guns at you.

You feel your friend go limp on your back. He's been hit. "Run. Save yourself," he whispers faintly. You scramble to get on your feet and dart toward a small group of trees.

Hundreds of Mexican soldiers were killed in the Battle of the Alamo. Others may have deserted the army to avoid injury or death.

Just then, you feel a sharp pain in your leg and chest. The bullet in your chest has hit your heart, and you collapse. Your effort to escape death by deserting the army has failed.

THE END

To follow another path, turn to page 11.
To read the conclusion, turn to page 101.

You care about your friend. But you must save your own life. You wrap his injured leg and cover him with your poncho. Then you sprint as fast as you can toward the rest of the group. They have already disappeared in the darkness.

You keep running but can't find them. You fear for your safety. How will you survive in the desert all alone?

A small grove of trees is nearby. You hide there and get some rest. As soon as the sun rises, you start moving again. You can't stay in one place too long. Either the Indians or the guards could find you.

The next night just before sunset, dark clouds roll in from the north. The temperatures drop quickly, and sleet begins to fall.

You search for food and for wood to start a fire. But you find neither. Your thin cotton uniform is wet and icy. Your hands are blue. Finally, you can go no farther. You collapse. As you drift off to sleep, you know this is your final resting place. You'll die alone here on the cold ground.

59

THE END

To follow another path, turn to page 11.
To read the conclusion, turn to page 101.

Colonel William Travis (forefront) led the Texian defenders at the Alamo.

CHAPTER 3

FIGHTING FOR TEXAS

You were born in Louisiana. You came to San Antonio 10 years ago to buy land and became a Mexican citizen. You paid your taxes and obeyed the laws.

But you no longer want to be a Mexican citizen. You think Santa Anna's strict laws are unfair, and you've joined with many other Texians in a fight for independence.

61

Since General Cos was defeated, rumors have buzzed around town. Some claim Santa Anna is marching north with an army of thousands.

Turn the page.

Davy Crockett joined the fight for Texas' independence.

Others say he won't come until spring. Just in case, you send your wife and children to Louisiana, where they'll be safe.

Nearly 150 men make up the garrison in San Antonio. Only a few men are trained soldiers. William Travis is one of the leaders. He shares command with Jim Bowie, who is one of your best friends.

A few men have joined the garrison from the United States. The other day, famous frontiersman Davy Crockett led a group from Tennessee into town.

Early in the morning on February 23, you are standing guard at San Fernando Church. Suddenly, you spot movement on the horizon. Hundreds of soldiers are marching from the south! The rumors were right. You yank the bell's rope. "Santa Anna is coming!" you yell.

Townspeople dash through the streets. Many flee the town. Others rush into the Alamo. Church leaders called missionaries lived in the Alamo about 100 years ago. Some buildings in the Alamo don't have roofs, and the tall walls surrounding the buildings are crumbling. But it's still the safest place to go.

Once inside the Alamo, you see Almaron Dickinson struggling with the cannons. Nearby, Travis is sending John Smith to the town of Gonzales to round up volunteers to help fight.

⇢ To help with the cannons, turn to page 64.

⇢ To help gather more Alamo defenders, turn to page 70.

You rush to Dickinson's side. "Is your family safely inside?" you ask.

"Yes, Susanna took baby Angelina into the sacristy," he says. The tiny sacristy is near the chapel. It's probably the safest place in the Alamo.

As you work on the cannons, more residents make their way into the Alamo. Some men lead cows into the back pen. Others cart corn into storage rooms. "We could be locked up in here for weeks," you mutter to yourself. "I'm glad we'll have plenty of food to eat."

Suddenly, you hear a child's cry for help. You peek through a small window. Eight-year-old Enrique Esparza is standing below you. The Alamo's front gates have already been locked and he can't get in. You lift him through the window. "*Gracias!*" he shouts, as he races to find his father, Gregorio — one of the volunteer fighters.

Many townspeople, including the Esparza family, rushed into the Alamo as the Mexicans neared.

Just then, William Travis approaches the cannons. "Santa Anna is here!" he cries, pointing to the San Fernando Church. The Mexicans have raised a red flag from the bell tower. When Travis sees it, he scowls. "Ha! Santa Anna wants us to surrender, but we're not giving up!" He pounds his fist on a cannon. "Fire it!" he orders. "We'll never surrender to that tyrant!"

Turn the page.

Dickinson loads the cannon. "Stand clear!" you shout as you pull the cannon's rope tight. Boom! Smoke rings rise as the iron ball soars through the air.

The Mexicans respond with cannonfire of their own. They continue firing throughout the evening. Luckily, they're still too far away to do any harm to the walls. Travis orders the cannon crew to fire only occasionally. The cannonballs can't be wasted this early in the attack. He knows they will be needed when the Mexicans move closer to the walls.

The next afternoon, Crockett stops you in the plaza. "Jim Bowie is very ill. They think it's typhoid fever," he says.

The Alamo

Gonzales (70 miles/113 km.)

North Gate

Where Col. Travis fell

Long Barracks

Cattle Pen

Horse Corral

The Chapel

Palisade defended by Davy Crockett

Officers' Quarters

Plaza of the Alamo

South Barracks

Guardhouse

Jim Bowie's Room

Alamo Headquarters

San Antonio (San Fernando Church, 800 yards/732 m.)

The 18 Pounder

Entrance to the Alamo

Goliad (95 miles/153 km.)

The Alamo included several rooms, which varied in size.

You hurry to Bowie's room. Along the way, a man stops you. "Travis wants us to gather supplies from the shacks in La Villita," he says, pointing to the nearby village. "Will you help us?"

➤ To get supplies from La Villita, turn to page **68**.

➤ To visit Bowie, turn to page **71**.

You agree to go. You push open the Alamo's heavy wooden gates. Then you sprint 300 yards to La Villita. You must move quickly so the Mexicans don't spot you. You search all the shacks and return with baskets of food, clothing, and blankets.

That night, the Mexicans continue shooting cannonballs at the walls. It seems like the explosions are getting louder and louder.

The next morning, you're patrolling back in the Alamo. You see a line of Mexicans marching into La Villita. You join a crew atop the wall, aim your rifle, and fire. The Mexican soldiers dive behind the shacks for cover. They return fire, but many have already been hit. The Mexicans retreat, dragging their wounded comrades with them.

Later, there is talk that Crockett needs help defending the south wall. You also hear that Travis wants men to burn La Villita so the Mexicans can't use the shacks for protection again.

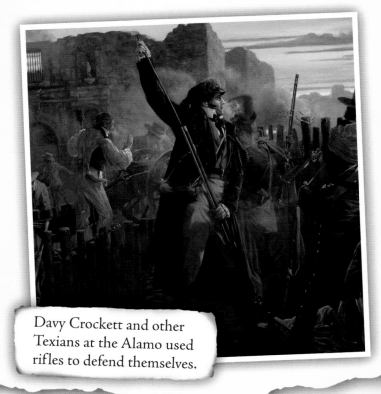

Davy Crockett and other Texians at the Alamo used rifles to defend themselves.

⟶ *To burn La Villita, turn to page **75**.*

⟶ *To help Crockett, turn to page **80**.*

You jump on a horse and gallop toward Smith. "I'll go with you to Gonzales," you say.

You charge through the gates. Dr. John Sutherland stumbles out behind you. "Wait!" he says. "I'll come too. I won't be able to help much here." Sutherland's leg was badly injured in a fall from his horse. He's in a lot of pain. But he still insists on riding to Gonzales with you.

It's 70 miles to Gonzales. You travel as many miles as you can before sunset. You arrive in Gonzales the next day at 4:00 in the afternoon.

After a few days, you have found several men who have agreed to help. You get ready to go back to San Antonio. But Sutherland is in too much pain to leave. "Will you stay and ride back with me later?" he asks.

➤ To return to the Alamo, turn to page 77.

➤ To stay with Sutherland, turn to page 88.

"I can't," you say. "I'm on my way to see Jim Bowie. He's very ill."

In a small room near the main gate, Bowie lies on a cot. He's dripping with sweat and coughing violently. "I can no longer lead the troops," he says. "I've told the men to obey Travis."

It's hard to see Bowie this way. He's always been so strong. He roped alligators as a child and became a brave fighter with his famous Bowie knife. You know he'd rather die fighting in battle than die from a disease.

Suddenly, Juan Seguín races up to Bowie. "I need to deliver messages for Travis so we can get more men to help us. Can I take your horse?"

Bowie agrees. Seguín might need help getting through enemy lines.

⇥ *To stay with Bowie, turn to page 72.*

⇥ *To go with Seguín, turn to page 78.*

You look at Bowie and decide to stay. After all, this might be the last chance you have to be with your friend.

All through the night, the Mexicans lob cannonballs at the walls. They're still not close enough to do much damage. But you fear it won't be long before they will be.

The next evening, you hear William Travis and Green Jameson talking.

"I just noticed that less water is flowing into the Alamo," Jameson says. "The Mexicans must be cutting off our water supply. We need men to dig a well inside the Alamo."

Jim Bowie became ill and was unable to leave his bed when the Mexicans attacked.

"We also need men to burn La Villita tonight," Travis replies. "The Mexicans are using the shacks for cover."

⇝ To dig the well, turn to page **74**.

⇝ To burn La Villita, turn to page **75**.

You start digging at the south end of the plaza. After an hour, you finally hit water. However, the digging has weakened a nearby parapet. This wall of soil was built to protect soldiers from enemy fire. It collapses in a heap. "Now we'll have no way to fire over this wall safely," Jameson says, shaking his head.

You spend several hours trying to repair the parapet. Later, a new crew comes to relieve you. On your way to the sacristy, you hear that Crockett needs help at the south wall. You decide to go.

74

Turn to page 80.

The jacales in La Villita quickly burst into flames.

You meet the other men at the gate. You light a torch and dart toward the small wooden shacks called jacales.

You touch your torch to the walls of one of the jacales. The shack bursts into flames. You move quickly through the village, lighting each jacale as you go. Soon, La Villita is a fiery scene.

Turn the page.

Across the river, the Mexicans see the flames. They aim and fire. Luckily, no one is harmed. Your crew is already back inside the Alamo.

On March 1, John Smith returns with 32 men from Gonzales. Travis is grateful they have come. Yet worry shows on his face. He's been sending out messages daily. So far, only the town of Gonzales has responded.

Two days later, you walk through the plaza. Smith is leaving to deliver a message to the Texian leaders in the town of Washington-on-the-Brazos. Green Jameson is gathering a crew to repair the crumbling north wall.

➤ *To repair the north wall, turn to page* **82**.

➤ *To go with Smith, turn to page* **92**.

"I'm sorry. I need to get back to the Alamo," you tell Sutherland. On your way back, you continue rounding up volunteers. On March 1, you enter the Alamo's gates with 32 men.

Travis is happy the men have come to help. But he had hoped Colonel James Fannin's army of hundreds would have come by now as well. Time appears to be running out. The Mexicans inch closer to the Alamo each day.

Two days later, you hear Smith and Green Jameson talking in the plaza. Smith is leaving to deliver a message to Texian leaders who are meeting in Washington-on-the-Brazos. You know the way to this town. Meanwhile, Green Jameson is looking for men to help him repair the crumbling north wall.

➤ To repair the north wall, turn to page 82.

➤ To go with Smith, turn to page 92.

"I'll return to see you later," you tell Bowie as you run out the door. You saddle your horse and gallop toward Seguín.

You ride east on Gonzales Road. In the distance, you see a soldier patrolling. Mexican cavalrymen stand near a fire. It's a roadblock.

As you approach, the patrolman orders you to stop. Seguín yells a greeting in Spanish. The soldier lowers his weapon. "He must think we're Mexicans," Seguín whispers. "We need to race by him before he realizes the truth."

You dig your spurs into your horse. Your horse bolts past the roadblock. The patrolman aims and fires, but he misses. Then the cavalrymen mount their horses and chase after you. But you've already escaped into the darkness.

Juan Seguín was a courier for
William Travis during the
Battle of the Alamo.

The next day, you help Seguín deliver
the messages. You're ready to go back to the
Alamo now. But Seguín wants to stay longer to
convince more men to help fight at the Alamo.

❖ To return to the Alamo, turn to page **90**.

❖ To stay with Seguín, turn to page **91**.

You walk toward the south wall. Crockett and his men are defending the palisade. This fence of tall sharpened logs forms the Alamo's outer wall near the church. It's meant to keep the enemy out. But it isn't as protective as a stone wall. It's definitely the weakest spot of the Alamo.

"I don't like being hemmed in," Crockett says. "I'd much rather take my chances fighting in the open."

"It does feel like a prison in here," you reply. "I fear it won't be long before the Mexicans attack."

Suddenly, you spot shadows near the river. Could it be Mexican soldiers? Crockett aims and fires his rifle. One of the figures goes down. Crockett is by far the best sharpshooter you've ever seen.

On March 1, Smith arrives back from Gonzales with 32 volunteers. Travis thanks them for coming. As he turns to walk back into his quarters, you see the worry on his face. You know he needs at least 50 times this many men to battle the Mexican forces successfully.

The Mexicans keep moving closer to the Alamo. By March 3, cannons have battered the north wall. Jameson needs men to repair it.

As you walk to the north wall to help, you see Smith saddling his horse. Travis has asked him to deliver more letters. One is to the Texian leaders who are gathered for a meeting in the town of Washington-on-the-Brazos. Another is a personal note.

→ To help repair the north wall, turn to page **82**.

→ To go with Smith, turn to page **92**.

You follow Jameson to the north wall. It's crumbling from the constant cannonfire. The Mexicans are now only about 250 yards away.

You must move quickly to stop the wall from caving in completely. You hammer wood braces and shovel dirt against the stone. After several hours, Jameson tells you to stop. "We've done the best we can for now," he says.

The next morning, you visit the sacristy with Gregorio Esparza. His children race to his side. Almaron Dickinson and his wife rock their baby to sleep. You spend the day there with your friends. You're grateful that your family is far away from this place.

On the afternoon of March 5, you return to help Jameson secure the north wall. Davy Crockett approaches. "Travis has ordered a meeting in the main plaza," he says.

As you enter the plaza, the bright sun warms your face. Everyone is here — the defenders, the women, and the children. Even Bowie is carried into the plaza on his cot.

Travis addresses the group. You can tell by the sad look on his face that he doesn't have good news. "I've sent many letters to the Texian leaders asking for help," he says. "Yesterday, I saw the Mexicans building ladders to climb the walls. I doubt any more volunteers will get here before they attack."

You study the faces in the crowd. They're all pale with worry. Everyone knows what a fight without more defenders means. It's impossible for fewer than 200 men to fight off thousands of soldiers.

Turn the page.

"I will fight to my last breath," Travis continues. He removes his silver sword from the sheath at his side. He uses it to cut a line in the sand. It stretches from one end of the plaza to the other. "Now you must decide. Cross the line if you want to stay and fight for the liberty of Texas."

Legend says Travis drew a line in the sand with his sword at the final meeting in the Alamo.

Davy Crockett, Almaron Dickinson, and Gregorio Esparza step across the line. Even Bowie is carried across the line on his cot. Within minutes, all have crossed the line except for you and a Frenchman named Louis Rose. "I can't stay and die here," Rose says. "This is not my war to fight."

You think of your own wife and children. You don't want to die, leaving them all alone. What would they do without you? Yet, your friends will need all the help they can get.

→ To cross the line, turn to page **86**.

→ To leave with Rose, turn to page **94**.

"Freedom means everything to me. I'll fight to the end," you say as you walk over the line.

You wish Louis Rose luck. So do the other men.

Later that evening, Susanna Dickinson prepares the evening meal. A gold cat's eye ring hangs on a chain around baby Angelina's neck. It's the one Travis always wears.

"It's a gift from Colonel Travis. He asked us to keep it safe for him," Susanna explains. "He hopes his ring will make it safely out of the Alamo, even though he doesn't believe he will."

It's late when you finally drift off to sleep. For the first night since you came into the Alamo, all is quiet. In the early morning hours of March 6, you're awakened by explosions. As you jump up to grab your rifle, you hear men shouting, "Viva Santa Anna!"

"They're attacking the north wall," Travis yells. He clutches his shotgun and saber, ready to fight.

You start to follow, but then you hear the women and children crying in the sacristy. Maybe you should check on them.

⇢ *To check on the women and children, turn to page* **96**.

⇢ *To follow Travis, turn to page* **98**.

"Sure," you say, waving to the other men as they leave. "I'll return in a few days."

After a week, Sutherland's leg does not improve. He tells you to go on without him.

You travel hard for two days. Finally, just before dawn on March 6, you approach the city.

You're still miles away, but your stomach sickens at what you see. The sky over the Alamo is filled with flashes of light. It looks like lightning. But you know it's not. With your hand-telescope, you see thousands of Mexicans charging to the Alamo's walls with ladders and muskets. You're witnessing a terrible battle.

Travis sent couriers to deliver letters throughout the Battle of the Alamo.

Your first instinct is to rush to the Alamo to help your friends. But you know there's nothing one man can do against thousands. If only you had a huge army with you. Then your friends in the Alamo might be saved.

All you can do is save yourself. You dig your spurs in your horse and race back toward Gonzales.

THE END

To follow another path, turn to page 11.
To read the conclusion, turn to page 101.

You don't want to stay. You leave immediately for the Alamo. You ride hard all day. When it gets dark, you know you should stop. There are many holes along this section of the road. And rain is pouring down. But you decide to keep going.

The rain pelts your face. It's cold and turning to sleet. But you only have a few miles left to travel before you reach San Antonio. You can't stop now.

Suddenly, your horse slips on the muddy road. You're launched forward, and the horse rolls on top of you. You scream in pain as your internal organs are crushed. Seconds later, you take your last breath.

THE END

To follow another path, turn to page 11.
To read the conclusion, turn to page 101.

You agree to stay with Seguín. The more men there are to defend the Alamo, the better.

You spend nine days rounding up volunteers. Some men agree to come. Others don't want to leave their families.

Just as you're about to return, your worst fears come true. You hear that the Mexican soldiers charged the Alamo in the early morning hours of March 6. All of your friends have died.

You cannot let this be the end. Later, you will join the army of Sam Houston. This famous Texian leader will keep fighting for Texas' independence. You vow never to forget the Alamo and your friends' fight for liberty.

THE END

To follow another path, turn to page 11.
To read the conclusion, turn to page 101.

"Wait, John, I'll go with you," you shout as you race to his side. You saddle a horse and sling a rifle over your back.

"I'll fire the cannon morning, noon, and night," Travis says. "That way you'll know we're still fighting."

The Alamo's gates creak open. To give you cover, a group of men sneak out and fire at the Mexicans on patrol. With the army distracted, you and Smith dig your spurs into your horses and race north.

You speed across the barren landscape, and stop only a few times to rest. When you finally reach Washington-on-the-Brazos, you're exhausted. You have traveled 200 miles in less than 57 hours. Still, it doesn't matter if you're tired. You must hurry and deliver the messages. Your friends' lives in the Alamo depend upon it.

You also search for volunteers to return with you. Fifty men agree to come. You begin heading back to the Alamo, but you can't travel as fast with 50 men.

When you arrive at Cibolo Creek, it's already the morning of March 10. As the horses drink, Smith presses his ear to the ground. He tries to hear the rumbling of the Alamo's guns. But all is silent.

Smith is worried. He sends a few men to ride closer to San Antonio. When they return, they tell you the horrible news. The Alamo has fallen. Your friends have all died trying to defend it. You will never forget the sacrifice they made for freedom.

THE END

To follow another path, turn to page 11.
To read the conclusion, turn to page 101.

You're sad at the thought of leaving your friends. But you must do what's best for your family. "I'm sorry, but I must leave too," you say.

You glance at the men around you. No one frowns upon you. They respect your decision. Travis thanks you for your service. Crockett and Bowie wish you luck.

As you prepare to leave that night, you look back one last time across the Alamo. Davy Crockett and his men are guarding the south wall. William Travis and Almaron Dickinson work on the cannons. Candlelight glows from Jim Bowie's room as he struggles to stay alive one more night. You hear the women in the sacristy softly talking. You believe this is the last time you'll see your friends alive.

The women and children stayed in the Alamo's tiny sacristy throughout the battle.

With this image burned in your memory, you climb over the tall stone wall and race into the darkness. You make it past the Mexican batteries without being detected. As you run northward to freedom, you know you've made it. You will see your family again.

THE END

To follow another path, turn to page 11.
To read the conclusion, turn to page 101.

You dash into the candlelit room. The women and children are crying. "No matter what you hear, don't leave this room," you say.

Back in the plaza, you think of Bowie. How will he defend himself? In his room, he lies on his cot, struggling for breath. He's too weak to fight. But by his side are two loaded pistols. His famous Bowie knife is resting on the table next to him. "Good luck, my friend," you yell as you run back into the plaza.

The Mexicans are charging from all sides now. Davy Crockett and his men fight at the south wall. Almaron Dickinson and Gregorio Esparza fire the cannons.

When you reach the north wall, you see a terrible scene. Lying on the ground is William Travis. He died — just as he said he would — defending the Alamo.

Jim Bowie designed his own knife. Today, Bowie knives are common hunting and camping knives.

The Mexicans are now pouring over the walls. You fire your rifle at them. But you're too late. Their bullets are already raining down upon you. Your battle is over. Just like Travis, you have given your life for the liberty of Texas.

THE END

To follow another path, turn to page 11.
To read the conclusion, turn to page 101.

You race behind Travis along the north wall. Cannonballs fly through the air. Suddenly, a bullet hits Travis. You look down and gasp in horror. He's dead.

"Crockett needs help," someone shouts. You leave Travis and dart across the plaza toward the south wall's palisade.

Hundreds of soldiers are climbing over the wall. Crockett and other defenders use hand-to-hand combat to defend themselves.

You rush to load your rifle, but it is too late. Mexicans with razor-sharp bayonets are charging toward you. There's no escape. Your last thoughts are of your wife and children as you collapse onto the soil.

THE END

To follow another path, turn to page 11.
To read the conclusion, turn to page 101.

When the Mexicans got inside the Alamo, both sides used hand-to-hand combat.

Today, thousands of people visit the Alamo to remember those who lost their lives there.

CHAPTER 4

REMEMBER THE ALAMO!

By dawn on March 6, the Battle of the Alamo was over. The Mexicans won. As he promised, Santa Anna did not take any prisoners. Every Texian defender inside the Alamo died in the battle. All of the women and children in the Alamo were allowed to leave.

The Mexicans tore down the Texians' flag. The Mexican red, white, and green battle flag was put up in its place.

Santa Anna wanted to make sure every defender was dead, especially the leaders. He demanded to see the bodies of William Travis, Jim Bowie, and Davy Crockett.

The Mexican soldiers searched the defenders' bodies for weapons and valuables. Then they heaped the bodies into a pile and burned them.

Texians weren't the only ones to die that day. Hundreds of Mexican soldiers were killed or wounded. Santa Anna would have lost far fewer men if he had waited for the 12-pound cannons to arrive. Many Mexican soldiers and officers lost respect for Santa Anna because of his decision to charge the Alamo before the larger cannons arrived.

Santa Anna ordered Alamo survivor Susanna Dickinson to carry a warning to Texian leader Sam Houston. If the other rebels did not surrender, they would share the same fate as their Alamo friends.

Susanna walked 70 miles east to Gonzales carrying her daughter, Angelina. When she arrived, she gave Houston the message. She also told him what she witnessed at the Alamo.

Houston ordered everyone to leave Gonzales. Then he burned the town and marched his army east toward San Jacinto.

Sam Houston prepared to battle the Mexican soldiers after the Battle of the Alamo.

Susanna Dickinson was a survivor of the Battle of the Alamo.

On April 21, Santa Anna and his men were resting near San Jacinto. Houston attacked and caught Santa Anna by surprise. As Houston's army charged, they shouted the battle cry, "Remember the Alamo!" The battle was over in 18 minutes. This time, the Texians won.

Santa Anna was caught during the battle, and he became Houston's prisoner. The Mexican leader begged for his life. Houston let him live, but not without a price. Santa Anna would have to order his armies back to Mexico and stay out of Texas forever. Santa Anna agreed. Texas was finally free.

The Republic of Texas remained its own country until 1845. That year, the Texian leaders decided to join the United States. Texas became the 28th state.

To this day, the people of Texas still remember the brave defenders of the Alamo. In fact, on the back of the state's seal is a sketch of the old mission's chapel. Above it is written Houston's battle cry from San Jacinto, "Remember the Alamo."

On April 21, 1836, Texians battled Mexican soldiers at the Battle of San Jacinto.

TIME LINE

1718 — The San Antonio de Valero Mission, later known as the Alamo, is one of three Texan missions established by Franciscan missionaries.

1793 — The king of Spain removes the San Antonio de Valero Mission from church leadership.

1802 — The San Antonio de Valero Mission is a military post.

1821 — Mexico wins independence from Spain.

1834 — Antonio López de Santa Anna becomes Mexico's president. Rebellions break out in Texas after Santa Anna makes new laws.

1835 —

October 9 — General Martín Perfecto de Cos arrives in San Antonio.

December 9 — General Cos surrenders to the Texians in San Antonio. Texians celebrate their victory, but know their fight isn't over.

1836 —

February 8 — Former Tennessee Congressman David "Davy" Crockett arrives with volunteers to defend the Alamo.

February 12 — William Travis is elected commander of the enlisted army forces at the Alamo, while Jim Bowie leads the volunteers.

February 23 — Santa Anna's Mexican army reaches San Antonio. Texian forces retreat inside the Alamo.

March 2 — Texian leaders sign the Texas Declaration of Independence in Washington-on-the-Brazos.

March 6 — Mexicans attack the Alamo before dawn, killing all inside except for the women, children, and Travis' slave. Mexican losses are around 600.

107

April 21 — The Texian army defeats the Mexican army and captures Santa Anna at the Battle of San Jacinto, winning independence for Texas.

1845 — Texas becomes the 28th state.

OTHER PATHS TO EXPLORE

In this book, you've seen how the events surrounding the Battle of the Alamo look different from two points of view.

Perspectives on history are as varied as the people who lived it. You can explore other paths on your own to learn more about what happened. Seeing history from many points of view is an important part of understanding it.

Here are some ideas for other Battle of the Alamo points of view to explore:

- The women and children inside the Alamo survived, but they had to live without their husbands and fathers. What do you think it was like to lose loved ones in the battle?

- Colonel William Travis sent out many couriers asking for help in defending the Alamo. What decision would you have made if a courier had asked you to help?

- Some people, such as Gregorio Esparza, were born in Mexico, yet sided with the Texian defenders. How do you think they were treated by those who were loyal to Santa Anna?

READ MORE

Doeden, Matt. *The Battle of the Alamo.* Mankato, Minn.: Capstone Press, 2005.

Fradin, Dennis Brindell. *The Alamo.* New York: Benchmark, 2007.

Schaefer, Ted, and Lola Schaefer. *The Alamo.* Chicago: Heinemann Library, 2006.

Walker, Paul Robert. *Remember the Alamo: Texians, Tejanos, and Mexicans Tell Their Stories.* Washington, D.C.: National Geographic, 2007.

INTERNET SITES

FactHound offers a safe, fun way to find Internet sites related to this book. All of the sites on FactHound have been researched by our staff.

109

Here's how:

1. Visit *www.facthound.com*
2. Choose your grade level.
3. Type in this book ID **1429613548** for age-appropriate sites. You may also browse subjects by clicking on letters, or by clicking on pictures and words.
4. Click on the **Fetch It** button.

FactHound will fetch the best sites for you!

GLOSSARY

battery (BAT-uh-ree) — a group of heavy guns that are all used together

cavalry (KAV-uhl-ree) — soldiers who fight on horseback

constitution (kon-stuh-TOO-shuhn) — the system of laws in a country that state the rights of the people and the powers of the government

garrison (GA-ruh-suhn) — a group of soldiers based in a town and ready to defend it

mission (MISH-uhn) — a church or other place where missionaries live and work

palisade (pal-uh-SAYD) — a fence of stakes built for defense

parapet (PA-ruh-paht) — an earthen or stone embankment protecting soldiers from enemy fire

saber (SAY-bur) — a heavy sword with a curved blade and one cutting edge

sacristy (SAK-ris-tee) — a room in a church containing holy objects

typhoid fever (TYE-foid FEE-vur) — a serious infectious disease with symptoms of high fever and diarrhea that sometimes leads to death

tyrant (TYE-ruhnt) — someone who rules other people in a cruel or unjust way

Bibliography

Davis, William C. *Three Roads to the Alamo.* New York: HarperCollins, 1998.

Hoyt, Edwin P. *The Alamo: An Illustrated History.* Dallas: Taylor, 1999.

John William Smith: Soldier, Messenger, Patriot. http://www.tamu.edu/ccbn/dewitt/smithjohnwilliam.htm

Lamego, General Miguel A. Sanchez, translated by Consuelo Velasco. *The Siege and Taking of the Alamo.* Santa Fe, N.M.: The Press of the Territorian, 1968.

Matovina, Timothy M. *The Alamo Remembered: Tejano Accounts and Perspectives.* Austin, Texas: University of Texas Press, 1995.

Nofi, Albert A. *The Alamo and the Texas War for Independence.* New York: De Capo Press, 1994.

Peña, José Enrique de la, translated and edited by Carmen Perry. *With Santa Anna in Texas.* College Station, Tex.: Texas A & M University Press, 1975.

Petite, Mary Deborah. *1836 Facts About the Alamo.* New York: De Capo Press, 1999.

Tinkle, Lon. *13 Days to Glory.* New York: McGraw Hill, 1958.

INDEX